PELÉ

PELÉ
Soccer Star & Ambassador

by Brian Trusdell

ABDO
Publishing Company

Published by ABDO Publishing Company, PO Box 398166, Minneapolis, MN 55439. Copyright © 2014 by Abdo Consulting Group, Inc. International copyrights reserved in all countries. No part of this book may be reproduced in any form without written permission from the publisher. SportsZone™ is a trademark and logo of ABDO Publishing Company.

Printed in the United States of America,
North Mankato, Minnesota
102013
012014

Editor: Chrös McDougall
Series Designer: Christa Schneider

Library of Congress Control Number: 2013946595

Cataloging-in-Publication Data

Trusdell, Brian.
 Pelé: soccer star & Ambassador / Brian Trusdell.
  p. cm. -- (Legendary athletes)
Includes bibliographical references and index.
ISBN 978-1-62403-132-8
1. Pele, 1940- --Juvenile literature. 2. Soccer players--Brazil--Biography--Juvenile literature. 1. Title.
796.334/092--dc23
[B]
                                        2013946595

TABLE OF CONTENTS

Pelé greets members of the US press corps at the 21 Club in New York upon signing with the New York Cosmos in 1975.

The Day US Soccer Changed

The scene in and around the 21 Club was a madhouse. Fifty-Second Street between Fifth and Sixth avenues in New York City was jammed. Cabs, trucks, and pedestrians all crowded around the entrance to the swank Manhattan restaurant.

Inside, photographers jockeyed in front of a small dais. They were all trying for a better position to get pictures of the main attraction—a 34-year-old, 5-foot-8 (173 cm) man from Brazil.

To the overwhelming majority of US residents in 1975, soccer was something foreigners played. This kind of mob was reserved for home run king Hank Aaron or New York Jets quarterback Joe Namath. But on June 10, 1975, the attention was all for a relatively slight Brazilian man that most people in the United States knew little of: Pelé.

The start time for the news conference neared. Officials inside the restaurant worried that the mob of photographers would overwhelm the stage. The photographers already were fighting,

The NASL

The NASL was formed in 1968 with the merger of two existing leagues, the United Soccer Association and the National Professional Soccer League. Both had begun play a year earlier and were the first coast-to-coast professional soccer leagues in the United States. The NASL started with 17 teams in four divisions. However, it plummeted to five teams in its second season and then eventually built to 20 teams by 1975, the year Pelé arrived. Four teams that play in Major League Soccer (MLS) today took their names from clubs that played in the NASL in 1975: the Portland Timbers, San Jose Earthquakes, Seattle Sounders, and Vancouver Whitecaps.

pushing, and shoving. Finally the event began. Photographers snapped countless pictures of a ceremonial contract signing between Pelé and the New York Cosmos of the North American Soccer League (NASL). Reporters fired questions at the guest of honor with machine-gun speed.

The excitement was all due to the magnitude of the moment: World soccer's biggest celebrity was coming out of retirement to play for a team few had ever heard of.

A Game for Sissies?

Soccer was at best a marginal sport in the United States in the mid-1970s. The attitude of many was summed up by longtime *New York Daily News* columnist Dick Young when he told fellow sportswriter David Hirshey, "Don't waste your time on soccer, kid. It's a game for Commie pansies."[1] It was an insult of the highest order, comparing soccer players and fans with communists and sissies.

Pelé signs his contract with the New York Cosmos at the 21 Club in New York. His wife Rosemeri, *in purple*, looks on.

Pelé's arrival in the United States was a major shock. He had been courted early in his career by the biggest teams in Europe such as Real Madrid of Spain. But he turned them down. He decided to play his entire career with the club he began with, Santos of Brazil.

Yet now he was coming out of retirement to play with a team few were aware of, in the NASL, in a country where few cared about the game.

Some NASL teams played in run-down stadiums. Like the Cosmos, their games were rarely shown on US television. And in 1975, the league averaged only 7,600 fans a game.

The swell of interest in Pelé was driven by curiosity and his international acclaim. Earlier in his career Pelé had helped Brazil win three World Cups. Soccer is the most popular sport in the world, and the World Cup is soccer's marquee event. The World Cup began in 1930, and it has been held every four years except for a 12-year break from 1938 to 1950 because of World War II (1939–1945). Yet through 1975, the United States had only competed in the World Cup three times.

Soccer in the United States

The birth of the modern game of soccer is attributed to a pub in England in 1863 when rules were first standardized for "association football." However, forms of the sport have been noted as far back as Roman times and even ancient China. In the United States, the Pilgrims reported seeing Indians play a football-type game called pasuckquakkohowog on a wide, sandy beach.

The first organized soccer team in the United States was founded in 1862 in Boston. Rutgers University beat Princeton University 6–4 in the first intercollegiate soccer game, played in 1869 in New Brunswick, New Jersey. Today that game is considered the first college football game. But by many accounts the game looked more like a mix between soccer and rugby.

An ill-fated attempt to launch professional soccer lasted one season with the American League of Professional Football Clubs in 1894. It was a six-team circuit from Boston to Washington. The US Soccer Federation was formed in 1913. The first professional league that lasted more than a year, the American Soccer League, began in 1921. Although restricted to the Northeast, it rivaled baseball and football in popularity until an internal struggle for control arose. The Great Depression, sparked by the stock market crash of 1929, eventually doomed the league two years later.

The last time was in 1950. US newspapers hardly noticed the team was there. And in 1975, the sport was still simply baffling to many Americans who associated soccer with sports such as cricket.

Pelé had retired from soccer in 1974. However, he came back for two primary reasons. One was that he was experiencing personal financial trouble fueled by bad investments. But he was also motivated by the suggestion that he was the one man who could change American attitudes about soccer. At the 21 Club, he told the throng of media:

An Unknown Sport

Americans were so uninformed about soccer in the 1970s, many people were unaware of the basic rules of the game or the custom that many Brazilian players went by one-name nicknames. "If you look at an old NASL game program, you'll notice a substantial number of pages devoted to explaining the game," said Jim Trecker, a former NASL public relations director.[3]

Association football—soccer, is the most widely played game in the world—except in the United States. It is my hope that I can help to make this game, which I love so much, as important a sport here as it is in the rest of the world.

After all, in Brazil, we have been importing knowhow from the United States for a long time. Now we're exporting a little bit.[2]

Risking a Reputation

Born into a poor family in a small Brazilian town, Pelé grew up playing soccer barefoot on the streets. The ball was made from a sock stuffed with rags or newspaper or a grapefruit. But he would play professionally and score his first goal when he was only 16. A year later, he would play in—and win—his first World Cup. Pelé would eventually be declared a national treasure by Brazil and become one of the greatest athletes of the 1900s.

Having achieved so much already, many wondered why Pelé would take such a gamble and risk the reputation he had earned. The United States was a country where baseball, American-style football, basketball, and ice hockey dominated. A contract for $2.8 million was part of the answer. That was an unheard-of sum at the time. But besides the money, Cosmos General Manager Clive Toye had spent four years trying to convince Pelé.

"And I could help the game of football there," Pelé wrote in his 1977 autobiography. "Toye had said so and he meant it, and I agreed."[4]

Now he was about to test whether the *jogo bonito*—the Portuguese phrase for "play beautifully"—style of play that he made famous with Brazil and that made him an international star would conquer the United States like it had the rest of the world.

Pelé signed with the New York Cosmos in 1975 in hopes of growing soccer in the United States.

Pelé's given name, Edson, was in tribute to Thomas Edison, who invented the light bulb.

What's in a Name?

Pelé was born Edson Arantes do Nascimento on October 23, 1940. Or was he? According to his official birth certificate, his name is Edison, and he was born on October 21. But Pelé has insisted throughout his life that official documents, including his passport, have always been wrong. It is a problem he attributes to Brazilian officials being "not so fussy about accuracy."[1]

Both Pelé and the government agree that he was born in Três Corações, a town approximately 185 miles (298 kilometers) northeast of Sao Paulo with a population of approximately 70,000 in 2013. Pelé was given his name as a tribute to a famous American: Thomas Edison. Since electricity came to Três Corações the same year Pelé was born, Pelé's father, Dondinho, named his son after the inventor of the light bulb.

The discrepancy over how to spell his first name hardly mattered, though, because nobody called him by either name. His family has called

Pelé's Full Name

Whether it is Edison or Edson, the rest of Pelé's name comes from the Portuguese/Brazilian convention of a given name plus two surnames, the mother's maiden name and the father's name. Edison or Edson was his given name while the rest of his name comes from his mother (Dona Celeste Arantes) and his father (Joao Ramos do Nascimento).

him "Dico" from birth. Dico is a common nickname for Edson, Pelé said. When he was older, he took on the nickname that the world knows him by today.

Soccer was a part of Pelé's life from the beginning because his father was a soccer player. However, Dondinho didn't make much money while playing for small semi-pro clubs. It often left the family in poverty and was a source of irritation between Dondinho and Pele's mother Dona Celeste, especially in a household that included Pelé's uncle Jorge; his grandmother; a sister, Maria Lucia; and a brother, Jair (or Zoca).

Dondinho's chance at a big contract came in 1942 when he signed with Atletico Mineiro in the city of Belo Horizonte, Brazil. But he injured his knee in his first game and returned to Três Corações. A series of moves to other small clubs followed. When Pelé was four the family relocated to Bauru. Settling in the rail hub of 90,000 people northwest of Sao Paulo not only meant a spot for Dondinho on the Bauru Athletic Club (BAC) team but also the promise of a civil servant's job.

Pelé presents his father, *right*, with a New York Cosmos jersey after Pelé's final game in 1977.

The non-soccer job was as a laborer in a medical clinic. That opportunity is what convinced Pelé's mother to agree to the move. She had unsuccessfully argued with her husband for years to give up soccer. The little money he made playing the sport convinced her it was an unreliable way to make a living, and she impressed that on young Dico. Much to her, and Dondinho's, dismay, the clinic job did not materialize until years after they arrived.

Pelé frequently could be found playing the game with a ball made from as big a sock as he could find stuffed with rags or newspaper. But he also was fascinated by the planes at the nearby airfield, the Aero Club, and was convinced he was going to be a pilot.

That was until one day when he and his friends were playing soccer near a hospital. When a ball went astray, they looked through the basement windows of the building and stumbled across an autopsy of a pilot who was killed in a crash. The sight of blood that had gushed from the corpse's mouth and the lifeless body made Pelé vomit, gave him nightmares, and scared him out of ever becoming a pilot.

> "For a long time after this experience I would wake at night, frightened by the nightmare of dreaming the scene over and over again, except that instead of the dead glider pilot on the table, it was me, my arm being raised and twisted, my blood pumping out of me to spurt against the already-stained wall to run down my cheek to soak my nightshirt and clog my throat and choke me."
>
> —*Pelé, writing in his 1977 autobiography about his nightmares after seeing the dead pilot*[2]

Birth of a Legendary Name

Dondinho saw Pelé's aspirations of becoming a pilot and tried to convince his seven-year-old son to concentrate his efforts on school, knowing reading and writing were essential tools. But seeing the dead body at age eight and having a disciplinarian for a teacher around the same time turned Pelé away from school and made him a poor student. Instead, his job as a shoeshine boy at the local train station and soccer took precedence.

It was also about this time when Dico earned the name Pelé. However, no one knows for sure, since he cannot remember exactly when or how he got the nickname, nor who gave it to him.

One explanation offered by New York-born Irish sportscaster Jimmy Magee is that an Irish priest working in the Bauru slums was watching Pelé and uttered the Irish words *"ag imirt peile."* That means "playing football" in Irish (Gaelic). Other children upon hearing the priest thought that he was calling the youngster by name and began to repeat it.

Pelé has said that was possible but unlikely. Another version told by Pelé was that the goalkeeper on his father's team at Vasco de Sao Lourenco was named Bile (Beh-LEY). While Dico mimicked Bile's antics in goal, he shouted "Bile," but as a three- or four-year-old it came out as "Pelé" (Peh-LEY). Of course, Pelé also has said he doesn't remember trying to say Bile.

And still another story comes from a friend from Bauru who suggested that one of the many Turkish businessmen who lived near Pelé's old neighborhood would say "pe" (Portuguese for foot) whenever Pelé accidentally touched the ball with his hand.

Regardless, Pelé hated the name, and it was the source of many fights. He grew angry with his friends for calling him that. But the angrier he got, the more his friends teased him. One fight earned him a two-day suspension from school.

"All I know is that from the time I was nine or so, I was Pelé to everyone I know, except to my family, who continue to call me Dico to this day," Pelé said.[3]

Elementary Soccer Education

Pelé began to accept the nickname in his late preteen years during a local tournament organized by the mayor of Bauru. He and his friends had formed a neighborhood team, Sete de Septembro (Portuguese for seventh of September). The team was named after

Nicknames

Calling Brazilian soccer players by one name, and not necessarily their given birth name, is very common and has no definite beginning. Some historians attribute the practice to the culture at large and the country's historically high illiteracy rate. Other scholars have written that single names might have originated in Brazil's slave system, which typically referred to slaves by one name. Slavery was abolished in the late 1800s.

When the English introduced the game to Brazil in the late 1800s, the practice of referring to players by their last name was common. But as the game grew in popularity, calling players by one name also became more prevalent. Seventeen players on Brazil's 23-man roster for the 2010 World Cup in South Africa went by one name.

a street near their homes. They usually played without shoes but needed cleats (or boots) to participate in the tournament. A local salesman and father of three of the boys on the team, Ze Leite, provided the shoes. Finally with proper footwear, the team, now renamed Ameriquinha (Little America), won the tournament at BAC's home stadium.

Pelé was the tournament's leading scorer, and he left the field that day with the crowd chanting "Pelé! Pelé!"

Dondinho, a center forward, often worked with his son, taking him to the abandoned field at the end of the street to drill him on specific skills, much to the chagrin of his mother. But Pelé continued to play, and in 1954, he began to get a taste of professional soccer. BAC was forming lower-division developmental teams, including a boys' team: Baquinho.

Brazil

Brazil is the largest and most populated country in South America. It is the fifth largest and fifth most populous country in the world. More than 200 million people live there. Colonized by Portugal in 1500, Brazil's dominant language is Portuguese. While the poverty rate has improved since Pelé's childhood, more than 20 percent of Brazilians are still poor. In 2011, the average monthly income was $631. Brazil's homicide rate was among the worst in the world. As a result, Fédération Internationale de Football Association (FIFA) and the International Olympic Committee were criticized for selecting Brazil as the host for the 2014 World Cup and Rio de Janeiro for the 2016 Olympic Games.

Invited to try out, Pelé was offered a contract. He remembered the contract being for an amount that was not much. But it was his first soccer paycheck.

It was also with Baquinho that Pelé met Waldemar de Brito, a former Brazilian national team member who had played in the 1934 World Cup. With De Brito as coach, Pelé and Baquinho won three Sao Paulo state youth championships.

All the while, Pelé was continuing to struggle in school, mostly he says for poor attendance. It took him two extra years to finish primary school. He dropped out after the fourth grade. But Baquinho's success led de Brito back to Sao Paulo to coach adults and attracted scouts to Bauru. One scout tried to lure Pelé to Rio de Janeiro, Brazil, and the Bangu club. While Pelé's mother refused to let him go, it didn't stop the scouts from coming. As Pelé grew older, more came until de Brito returned from Sao Paulo.

Well aware of young Pelé's skills, de Brito lobbied a similar-minded Dondinho and a skeptical Dona Celeste until she relented. De Brito convinced Pelé's mother that he had already spoken to the owner of Santos Football Club (FC) and would watch over the boy. Pelé, then 15, was ecstatic at an opportunity for a pro contract; his mother thought it was a mere tryout.

It was a moment that would change the course of soccer history.

Pelé, *shown in 1965,* wears the uniform of his longtime club team, Santos FC.

CHAPTER 3

Pelé had never been to a big city until arriving in Sao Paolo, Brazil, in 1956.

To Sao Paulo, Santos, and Sweden

Still only 15, Pelé was embarking on the biggest journey of his life. Rarely out of the watchful sight of his parents, especially his mother, he was leaving the relatively small town of Bauru for the metropolis of Sao Paulo. As it was in 1956, Sao Paulo is the financial and economic center of the country. Today the metro area has a population estimated at 20 million.

The young Pelé had been too young to have many vivid memories of Três Corações. And he had never traveled much farther than Bauru. So he had little knowledge outside his small world.

Now he was on a train, leaving from the very station where he spent his youth shining shoes. With his father accompanying him, they rode approximately 180 miles (290 kilometers) into the state capital, one of the largest cities in the world. Waldemar de Brito was there waiting for them. From there, it was a 50-mile (80-kilometer) bus ride to Santos and Pelé's first look at the Atlantic Ocean.

His arrival on a Sunday coincided with a home game for Santos FC against Comercial in the Sao Paulo state championship. Pelé had grown up as a fan of Corinthians from Sao Paulo. He followed their games on the radio and in newspapers. But from his first moment at Estádio Urbano Caldeira, better known as Vila Belmirio stadium because of the Santos neighborhood where it is located, Pelé became a Santos FC fan.

Pelé was given a bunk in an eight-bed room in the stadium, where many of the single players lived. Within days he was training with the senior team, quickly earning praise and gaining a reputation as a talented player. But he still had to play with the club's Under-20,

Santos FC

The Santos Football Club (Santos FC) was founded in 1912 and had some success before Pele's arrival. It won the Sao Paulo state championship in 1935 and again in 1955 and 1956, the years immediately before Pelé began playing regularly for the team. However, its most successful years were clearly during Pelé's era. Through 2013, the team had won 20 Paulista crowns. Half of them came during Pelé's time with the club. The Paulista is the Sao Paulo state championship.

Santos also won six of its eight national championships during Pelé's time, plus two of three South American club championships, and both Intercontinental Cups.

The team has called Estadio Urbano Caldeira, named after a former player, home since 1916. Also known as Estadio Vila Belmiro for the neighborhood in which it is located, it had its peak capacity of approximately 33,000 in the mid-1960s. It was renovated and now has a capacity of almost 16,000.

U-18, and U-16 teams. He helped the U-20 team to the Sao Paulo state youth championship.

Pelé's early play eventually earned him a contract for 6,000 cruzeiros (a currency no longer in use) a month, although he said it was not "strictly legal" because of his age.[1] It only took a few months before Santos manager Luis Alonso Perez, better known as Lula, gave Pelé his chance with the senior team.

Pelé stepped out onto the field against Corinthians of Santo Andre on September 7, 1956. As if a touch of fate or coincidence, that date was Brazilian independence day and also the name of the neighborhood club team (Sete de Septembro) Pelé founded with his friends. The game was a friendly, or exhibition, and Pelé didn't enter the game until the second half.

State Championships

Unlike most other countries, Brazil's club soccer season has two equally important parts, the national and state championships. Because of soccer's popularity and the large number of clubs, each state or province in Brazil has its own championship. These are played during the first half of the calendar year. Because of the size of Brazil and its transportation infrastructure, until 1959, only the state championships existed. The most important of the state championships are in the two biggest provinces, Rio de Janeiro (called the Carioca) and Sao Paulo (the Paulista). The national championship, the Brasileiro, is played in the second half of the year. Both are played in a league format, similar to US sports. This is different from European countries, which play a cup, or single-elimination tournament, at the same time as the national league championship.

Shortly after replacing Del Vecchio in the lineup, Pelé converted the rebound of a shot by Pepe and had his first goal for a professional team. Such a debut in a 7–1 victory only furthered the rapidly growing reputation of the youngster. Two months later he scored again in his second match for Santos in a 4–2 victory over Espanha. By the first half of 1957, he had regular playing time with the senior first team.

A new contract for an extra 1,000 cruzeiros a month came on April 8, 1957. But it wasn't until the summer when Pelé's fame started to build outside of Sao Paulo.

Noticed at a Higher Level

Pelé was chosen to be part of a team made up of players from Rio de Janeiro's Vasco da Gama club and Santos FC for an exhibition tournament in Rio's famous Estadio Maracana. The tournament included four Brazilian teams and four from Europe.

Pelé scored three goals against Belenenses of Portugal in a 6–1 win. He added another against Dinamo Zagreb of Yugoslavia to earn a 1–1 draw. Then he scored one more against Flamengo of Rio de Janeiro in a second 1–1 draw. It was a performance that days later earned him a call from the Brazilian national team to play a pair of games against archrival Argentina.

In the first game, also at Maracana, Pelé again entered as a substitute for his Santos teammate Del Vecchio. And Pelé scored to tie the game at 1–1. However, Argentina ultimately prevailed 2–1. Three days later, Pelé made the starting lineup for the game in Sao Paulo. He scored in the 18th minute and led Brazil to a 2–0 victory. The win gave Brazil the Copa Roca, or Roca Cup, a series of games played irregularly between Argentina and Brazil since 1914. It is named after the former president of Argentina, Julio Roca, who urged the competition and donated the trophy given to the winner.

The impression Pelé left with the Brazilian national team coaches, including manager Vicente Feola and selectors, was a lasting one. As 1957 progressed, Pelé became the regular "No. 10" forward for

Estadio Maracana

Built for the 1950 World Cup, Estadio Maracana takes its popular name from the Rio Maracana, a river in Rio de Janeiro. However, the stadium is formally named Estadio Jornalista Mario Filho for a local reporter who lobbied for its construction. It was filled to capacity for the 1950 World Cup final between Brazil and Uruguay. The attendance is listed as 173,850. Other estimates for the game were 199,854, with some as high as 210,000. Reduced in capacity to approximately 80,000, it is now used by Rio de Janeiro soccer clubs Botofogo, Flamengo, Fluminense, and Vasco da Gama. It was used for the 2007 Pan American Games and also is being renovated for the 2014 World Cup and 2016 Olympic Games.

Santos and scored 17 goals in the Sao Paulo state championship season. In soccer, the No. 10 jersey is often worn by the team's creative midfielder/forward. In addition to scoring goals, this player directs the offense much like a quarterback in American football.

With the new year and the 1958 World Cup in Sweden approaching, every player tried that much harder to be considered for Brazil's *selecao*. That is the Portuguese word for selection, or national team.

By May, when the final choices for the roster were made, Pelé was picked over well-known stars such as Luzinho of Corinthians. It was a major step, but Pelé still had three preparatory matches before leaving for Sweden. He scored twice in a 5–1 win over Paraguay and added two more goals in 3–1 victory over Bulgaria.

The final prep match was against Corinthians. Ari Clemente of Corinthians attempted a tackle and hit Pelé's right knee, sending him to the ground. Pelé got up and tried to put weight on the knee, but it immediately buckled. Team doctors immediately assured Pelé that he would be all right and could go to the World Cup. But as he limped in the following days, he worried about whether he would make the trip.

He had reason to worry. Unbeknownst to him at the time, team officials were considering replacing him with Almir, a midfielder from Vasco da Gama.

Pelé's fear of flying still lingered from his childhood, but he was relieved when he boarded the plane to Europe. The team first flew to Italy for two more friendlies against club teams Fiorentina and Internazionale before continuing on to Sweden. Pelé sat out both games in Italy while team officials considered sending him home.

The World Stage

The Brazilian team arrived in Sweden six days before the first game. But Pelé still was not well enough to play. He was kept out of the opening games against Austria, which Brazil won 3–0, and England, which ended in a 0–0 draw. But slowly Pelé was included in the practice sessions. And by the final training session before Brazil's final group game against the Soviet Union, he was playing with the first team.

FIFA

FIFA is a French acronym for Fédération Internationale de Football Association, which translates to the International Federation of Association Football (or soccer). It is the governing body for the sport throughout the world and regulates soccer through six geographic regional confederations and 209 national associations, such as the US Soccer Federation (USSF) and Brazilian Football Confederation (CBF). FIFA runs the World Cup for both men and women. It also runs the soccer tournaments at the Olympic Games as well as world championships at the U-20 and U-17 levels, futsal (also known as five-a-side or indoor), and beach soccer.

Stepping onto the field in Gothenburg, Sweden, Pelé at age 17 became the youngest player to actually play in a World Cup game. Vava scored two goals, and Brazil beat the Soviets 2–0 to advance to the quarterfinals.

It was against Wales that Pelé's international fame exploded. After a scoreless first half, Pelé scored one of the World Cup's most replayed goals in the 66th minute. With his back to the goal in the penalty area, he trapped a ball off his chest, chipped it past Wales midfielder Mel Charles, pivoted around Charles, and volleyed the ball after it bounced once. The ball sailed into the back of the net before Welsh defender Stuart Williams or goalkeeper Jack Kelsey could block it.

Pelé ran into the goal, fell to his knees over the ball, and was mobbed by his teammates. Photographers ran onto the field to capture the moment.

"And the goal was, perhaps, the most unforgettable of my career," Pelé said. "It boosted my confidence completely. The world knew about Pelé. I was on a roll."[2]

Brazil came into the 1958 World Cup with past success. The team had reached at least the quarterfinals in 1938, 1950, and 1954. But entering the 1958 tournament, the European press often characterized Brazil and its team made up of predominantly black

The Brazilian national team poses before the 1958 World Cup final against Sweden. Pelé is in the front row, third from the left.

players as talented but undisciplined and without the drive of their European counterparts.

But Pelé and his teammate Garrincha were changing that perception. Five days after playing Wales, Pelé scored three second-half goals against France to seal a 5–2 victory in the semifinals. That sent Brazil to the championship game for the first time since a memorable loss to Uruguay in the 1950 World Cup at Maracana. Pelé remembered his father inviting his friends over to the house to listen to that 1950 game on the radio, and then seeing Dondinho crying afterward. Pelé promised his dad he would win a World Cup for him someday, and now he was in position to fulfill that pledge.

But it would be difficult. Brazil would be playing host Sweden. The game was at Rasunda Stadium on the outskirts of Stockholm, before a very partisan crowd including the King of Sweden.

Nils Liedholm gave Sweden the lead in the fourth minute, but Vava tied the score for Brazil five minutes later. Vava put Brazil ahead with his second goal in the 32nd minute. Pelé secured the lead in the 55th minute. He beat two defenders and put a shot past goalkeeper Kalle Svensson to make the score 3–1.

Mario Zagallo added a fourth goal for Brazil in the 68th minute. Agne Simonsson tried to rally Sweden with a tally in the 80th. But it was too late. Pelé lofted a header just out of the reach of Svensson in the 90th minute to cap a 5–2 victory and earn Brazil its first World Cup title.

Pelé cried. His teammates carried him on their shoulders. With the victory, Brazil became the first non-European team to win a World Cup in Europe. For almost any other player, it was a World Cup performance that would be more than enough to assure a place in soccer history. For Pelé, however, it was only a beginning.

A Brazil teammate hugs Pelé after their team won its first World Cup championship in 1958 in Sweden.

CHAPTER 4

Pelé, shown in 1958, was an international sports star after helping Brazil win the 1958 World Cup.

Making Santos into a Power

The praise, parties, and gifts for the Brazilian national team did not stop for weeks after the World Cup. Photographs, headlines, and stories about the players—in particular Pelé, the 17-year-old star from Santos FC—were splashed across the world.

When the team's plane first touched down in Brazil, in the eastern city of Recife, a throng awaited the players in the pouring rain at the airport. The crowd roared as the players emerged from the plane. The fans carried the players on their shoulders—even though the players had only landed for a refueling stop.

The fanfare continued as the team flew on to Rio de Janeiro. Fans lined the streets in every direction as far as the eye could see, cheering as the players were paraded through the streets on fire trucks.

Even more crowds greeted the team in Sao Paulo. Pelé and Santos teammates Zito and Pepe were even further celebrated when they returned

Transfers

Transfers are the most common way players move from club to club within soccer. For a player whose contract has not expired, one team will purchase the player's contract from another club for a fee. Typically a player receives a portion of the fee as a bonus. The player and the new club almost always negotiate a new contract. In most cases, all three parties—both clubs and the player— agree to all of the terms of the transfer before it is completed. If a player's contract has expired, he can move to another club on a "free transfer." This is comparable to the US custom of signing as a free agent.

to the club. When Pelé finally got home to Bauru, the town turned out en masse, and he was given a car, albeit a three-wheeled Romi-Isetta. It was much more modest than the convertible he was hoping for. It was of little consequence, though, since he did not have a driver's license. He left the car in Bauru for his father to drive.

Eventually, the hoopla subsided, and Pelé had to get back to the reality of his day job, Santos FC. He might have been known throughout the world now, but he wasn't even the best-paid player on his club team. Still, his goal-scoring prowess continued. Del Vecchio had been transferred to Verona in Italy. That meant Pelé was now the club's main scoring threat.

By midseason of the 1958 Sao Paulo state championship, Santos had won many games handily. Santos won 10–0 over Nacional, 8–1 over Guarani, 8–1 over Ypiranga, 9–1 over Comercial, and back-to-back 7–1 wins over Juventus and Guarani. Pelé scored 58 goals in 38 games as Santos won the 1958 Paulista title by four points over Sao Paulo FC.

A new contract with Santos enabled Pelé to buy his parents' home for them. And Santos, which had won three Paulista titles in four years, had a star attraction that it wanted to market.

International Demand

The club began to tour internationally in the off-season, traveling to play teams in other parts of the world such as the Americas and Europe. It began a period when Santos, and Pelé, would play dozens of extra games per year. Pelé said he played 103 total games in 1959. Fans around the world wanted to see Santos and the great Pelé.

In mid-1959, a European tour from May to early July included stops in Bulgaria, Belgium, the Netherlands, Italy, West Germany, Switzerland, Spain, Portugal, and Austria. The period coincided with Pelé's year of mandatory service in the Brazilian military and the early stages of a romance with the woman who would become his first wife. But the games, the goals, and the titles continued.

With Pelé, Santos won five Paulista championships between 1960 and 1965. They won the newly created Brazilian national championship five straight times from 1961 and 1965. And Santos won the tournament

Points System

From the beginning, soccer leagues used the standard of two points for a victory, one for a draw, and zero for a loss. That began to change when England adopted the contemporary three points for a victory in 1981. The idea was to encourage teams to try to win, rather than not lose. More and more leagues began to adopt the change. After the 1990 World Cup, which was criticized for its overly defensive, boring play, FIFA adopted the rule for all of its tournaments.

between the top clubs in the Rio de Janeiro and Sao Paulo states four times between 1959 and 1966. In all, Santos won 10 Paulista titles and six national championships during Pelé's reign. And that was just within Brazil.

Internationally Santos won the Copa Libertadores, or South American club championship, in 1962 and 1963, becoming the first Brazilian team to win the crown. Those titles qualified Santos for the Intercontinental Cup between the South American and European champions. It won both, in 1962 and 1963.

Pelé's success at the club level confirmed his World Cup heroics, and soon he was being sought after by European teams. Internazionale and Juventus in Italy made offers, but neither Pelé nor Santos was interested.

Hoping to ward off any further interest, in 1961 Brazilian President Janio Quadros had declared Pelé a national treasure. That designation technically prohibited anybody, such as a foreign soccer team, from exporting Pelé to play there.

Pelé shakes hands with Omar Sivori, a player for Juventus in Italy, during a European tour with Santos in 1961.

Santos, especially its 1962–63 team, was considered by some as the best club team of all time. Along with Pelé, the team featured players such as Zito, Pepe, Coutinho, and Gylmar. Santos was in constant demand internationally and toured worldwide repeatedly throughout the 1960s.

Money, Fame, Trouble

After the 1958 World Cup, Pelé began to make more money, not only from new contracts with Santos but from endorsements. Many companies paid Pelé to use and endorse their products, from trousers to soft drinks. His salary after 1959 rose to 80,000 cruzieros a month with a 60,000 cruziero living allowance. That figure was equal to approximately $75,000 to $100,000 per year.

The fame and popularity of Pelé grew steadily. US Senator Robert Kennedy visited Pelé in the Santos

Championship Tournaments

The Copa Libertadores de America, or Liberators of America Cup, is the South American club championship. Played annually since 1960, it pits the best teams of the 10 South American leagues against one another. The tournament is the continent's version of the European Champions League. It is named for the leaders of the movements that gained independence from Europe for the various South American nations. The winner qualifies for the FIFA Club World Cup, a competition between the various continental club champions.

From 1960 to 2004, the winner qualified for the Intercontinental Cup, sending it to a game against the European champion. Since those two continents dominated world soccer, the winner was considered the best club team in the world. Between 1980 and 2004 the Europe-South American matchup was a single-game championship played in Tokyo, Japan, as the Toyota Cup, named after the Japanese car company that sponsored it. It has been replaced by the FIFA Club World Cup.

locker room in 1965. Pelé met Pope Paul VI in 1966. Zaire (now called Democratic Republic of the Congo) gave Pelé the key to the city of Kinshasa when Santos toured in Africa in 1967. And Pelé played a match at Maracana for England's Queen Elizabeth II in 1968.

In January 1969, while Santos was on a tour of Africa, the two warring sides in the Nigerian civil war (also known as the Nigerian-Biafran War) reportedly agreed to a 48-hour truce to allow the club to play an exhibition match. Pelé said he wasn't sure of the ceasefire but remembered seeing tanks and a large security presence in Lagos, Nigeria, for the match against Stationery Stores FC.

Later that year, Pelé scored his 1,000th goal. It was on a penalty kick against Vasco da Gama. A crowd of 80,000 fans witnessed the goal at Maracana in a driving rain.

Three years earlier, Pelé had married Rosemeri dos Reis Cholbi after eight years of courtship. The wedding was seen by some as controversial since he was black and Rosemeri was white. As in the United States at the time, the races were very much segregated in Brazil and interracial marriages were virtually unheard of.

Pelé's heyday with Santos came with off-the-field strife. In 1960, upon the advice of teammate Zito, Pelé had invested some of his money with Jose Gonzales Ozoris, better known as Pepe Gordo (or Fat Pepe).

Rosemeri dos Reis Cholbi

Only months removed from the 1958 World Cup, Pelé met the woman who became his first wife. It was the night before a game against Corinthians while Santos FC was in training camp. He and several of his teammates went to watch a girls' basketball game between a local team and the Corinthians team. Rosemeri, 14 at the time and three years younger than Pelé, was playing for the Santos team Atletico Santista. The two struck up a conversation. Pelé would later learn that she didn't "really like football."[1]

The principal investment that he involved Pelé in was a building materials company called Sanitaria Santista. A year later the company expanded into construction. Having seen his father struggle as a soccer player and having watched teammates have their careers ended by injuries, Pelé was happy to have an insurance plan.

But due to benign neglect and trust in Pepe Gordo, Sanitaria Santista did poorly. By 1965, Pelé was being chased by creditors. He was, in essence, broke and in debt.

Unwilling to accept the shame of bankruptcy, Pelé went to the directors of Santos FC for help. They agreed to pay off his debts as part of a new contract that paid him substantially less than what he otherwise would have made. He was finally clear of his debts by 1969. But it was a lesson that would need to be repeated and that would force him down a path that would further define his life and career.

Newlyweds Pelé and Rosemeri dos Reis Cholbi are welcomed with flowers at the airport in Munich, Germany, at the start of their honeymoon in 1966.

CHAPTER 5

Pelé and other Brazil fans had high expectations going into the 1962 World Cup in Chile.

Cementing a Legacy

Brazil's approach to the 1962 World Cup was similar to the one four years earlier. Team officials tried to duplicate the training and preparation in hopes that repetition would produce the same victorious results.

The coach had changed from an ailing Feola to Aimoré Moreira. But nine of the players who were on the field for the 1958 final in Stockholm, Sweden, including Pelé, made the trip to Chile for the 1962 World Cup. Many of the 1958 staff members returned as well.

The training regimen remained the same under conditioning coach Paulo Amaral. The general team rule was that players needed to take part in the daily workouts or they were ineligible to play in the games.

In the weeks before the start of the World Cup, Brazil played four friendly matches, two each against Portugal, and Wales. Pelé played in all four but felt a twinge in his groin after the first match.

Though he scored four goals in the games, the pain grew progressively worse.

He was fit enough to start at the World Cup. And in the opening game he and Zagallo each scored a goal to lead Brazil past Mexico 2–1. After the game he went to the team physician, Dr. Hilton Gosling. Gosling considered excusing Pelé from training. But knowing the consequences of that decision, Pelé lied about the seriousness of the pain.

The next game was against Czechoslovakia. At one point Pelé shot the ball into the post. Pelé got the rebound and attempted another shot. It was then that he felt his groin give way. He immediately fell to the ground in pain. He limped off, but because substitutions were not allowed at the time, he returned to finish the match.

Brazil and the Czechs played to a 0–0 draw. Regardless, that was the end of Pelé's World Cup. Barely able to walk, Pelé tried to convince the doctor to give him an injection to mask the pain.

"As if you were a horse? No, Pelé—you're talking to the wrong man," Gosling told him. "If I gave you an injection and you played, you could be crippled for life. And that would end your career in football. Do you think it would be worth it? What made you think I would allow such a thing?"[1]

Pelé watched on television while his replacement, Amarildo, scored twice in the final 20 minutes to rally Brazil to a 2–1 victory over Spain. Treatment and recovery were slow. Pelé was unavailable for both the quarterfinal victory over England and the semifinal win over host Chile. Pain-free three days before the championship game against Czechoslovakia, Pelé trained with the rest of the team. That was until he attempted a corner kick, and the pain immediately shot through his body. He had reinjured the groin.

> "I've always been religious. I come from a Catholic family, full of faith and always looking for God along my paths through life. When I was a child I wasn't allowed out to play with the other boys unless I went to Mass at Santa Terezinha church. I had to keep the customs my parents kept; as a child I became religious through these customs. . . . God has given me a talent, and I have always felt an obligation to develop it for good things."
> —*Pelé, as written in his autobiography*[2]

Brazil went on to win a second World Cup, this one without Pelé. Brazil beat Czechoslovakia 3–1 in the final.

Pelé would not return to full health for two months, but when he did, his fears of his career being finished were dismissed. He helped Santos win the Copa Libertadores, the Paulista, and the Intercontinental Cup. He scored two goals in a 3–2 victory over Benfica of Portugal in the first leg of the

Bulgaria's goalie punches the ball away before Pelé, *in back*, or his Brazil teammate can get a head on it in the 1966 World cup.

Intercontinental Cup at Maracana. Then he added three more in the second leg, a 5–2 win in Lisbon, Portugal.

"After the disappointment in Chile, it was like starting a new life," Pelé said.[3]

A Brutal 1966

By the time the 1966 World Cup in England began, Pelé was a nine-year veteran professional who had traveled the globe several times over, including for two

World Cups. Instead of being an unknown teenager, now he was an established threat at age 26. Teams devised tactics and strategies specifically to thwart Pelé and fellow Brazil star Garrincha.

The 1966 World Cup became known for its defensive and sometimes brutal play. Even free-flowing Brazil had adopted some of the defensive methods. Man-marking was common, including a physical style of play that would usher two significant changes four years later: substitutions and yellow cards/red cards.

As the two-time defending champion and with Feola still in place again as manager, Brazil entered the World Cup as a heavy favorite. But that only served to feed overconfidence, especially with an aging roster.

Brazil's opening match was against Bulgaria. Pelé and Garrincha both converted free kicks for goals to lift Brazil to a 2–0 victory. But Pelé was marked by Dobromir Zechev, whose physical play left Brazil's star with an injured leg.

"I kept getting tripped up and kicked to pieces, especially by Zhechev [sic], who seemed to mistake my ankles for the ball," Pelé recalled in his autobiography. "He didn't stop kicking me, and the referee did nothing to protect me or my team-mates [sic] from these rough-house tactics."[4]

Feola and Brazil's coaching staff replaced the hobbling Pelé with Tostao in the next game against

Hungary. Hungary, inspired by Florian Albert's two second-half goals, prevailed 3–1. That put Brazil in the position of needing a lopsided victory against Portugal in its last group match. Otherwise, it would be eliminated.

A still ailing Pelé was reinserted into the starting lineup, and Manga replaced Gilmar in goal. But an apparently nervous Manga allowed two goals in the first 27 minutes, and Portugal's Morais brutalized Pelé to the point where he limped off the field and vowed never to play in another World Cup.

"I don't want to finish my life as an invalid," he said after the 3–1 loss.[5]

1970 and Another Trophy

It took two years after his 1966 experience before Pelé donned the yellow shirt of Brazil again. And it was another year after that before he considered taking back his pledge not to play in another World Cup.

By then, Pelé had made his first trip to the United States in August 1966 and saw the birth of his first child, Kelly Cristina, in January 1967. In 1968, Pelé scored 59 goals in 81 games and Santos won five titles. A year later, Pelé had begun to rebuild his finances with a business agent, Marby Ramundini.

He had been given a part in a daytime drama, or telenovela, and was earning a lot of money endorsing

Pelé lies in agony after a slide tackle injured him while playing
Portugal during the 1966 World Cup in England.

Substitutions

For the first time, the 1970 World Cup allowed substitutions. Although the first rules of soccer written in 1863 did not permit replacement players, gradually they were allowed in different parts of the world at different times. The International Football Association Board, soccer's official rule-making body, first acknowledged substitutes in 1932. The board expanded the rule to permit replacements for an injured goalkeeper and another hurt player in 1958. However, Pelé made his first professional appearance as a substitute in 1957. England didn't allow substitutes until 1965. By 1967, two substitutes were allowed by FIFA, regardless of injury. That would increase to two plus a goalkeeper by the 1994 World Cup, and in 1995 to the current rule of three regardless of position or injury.

a wide range of products, including shoes, sporting goods, and coffee.

It all was leading him to consider another run at the World Cup. With reporters now blaming Brazilian soccer officials for much of the 1966 failure, the team management was overhauled over the next several years. In addition, the World Cup also was to be played in Mexico, which was closer to Brazil and had a more similar climate than Europe.

Pelé scored six goals in qualifying and helped Brazil win all six games by a combined 23–2 to easily make the 16-team field. Now he was ready to go back to the World Cup. A change in manager from former journalist Joao Saldanha to Pelé's 1962 teammate Mario Zagallo shortly before the World Cup didn't keep Brazil from entering the tournament as a 7–2 favorite.

The 1970 World Cup was the first to be broadcast on color television around the world. And Brazil, in its bright yellow shirts, put on a signature display of *jogo bonito*. Despite falling behind early in its opener against Czechoslovakia, Brazil rallied for a 4–1 victory. Pelé scored one of the goals in the second half. A Jairzinho strike gave Brazil a 1–0 win against England in the next game. Then Pelé scored twice to lead his side over Romania 3–2 in the final game of the first round.

World Cup

The 1970 World Cup was a much bigger occasion than the first World Cup. The tournament began in 1930 as a true world championship. Prior to then, the only other world championship tournament was the Olympics, but the Olympics was limited to amateurs. So in 1930, FIFA held the first World Cup in Uruguay. But with intercontinental travel still mostly restricted to steamships, only 13 teams played. The 1934 World Cup had 16 teams. The tournament consistently grew more popular after that until World War II forced the cancellation of the 1942 and 1946 events.

The tournament grew rapidly during the 1960s and 1970s. During that time, improvements in technology allowed games to be broadcast on television and eventually in color. The tournament also grew bigger, jumping from 16 teams to 24 in 1982.

Today the World Cup is a massive global event. The tournament expanded to 32 teams in 1998. According to FIFA, nearly 3.2 billion people, in every country on the planet, watched the 2010 World Cup in South Africa. When qualifying began for the 2014 World Cup, 204 nations entered in hopes of being one of the final 32.

Yellow Cards and Red Cards

The introduction of yellow and red cards at the World Cup also came into use in 1970 after some confusion during the tournament four years earlier. In the match between England and Argentina, German referee Rudolf Kreitlein ejected Argentina captain Antonio Rattin and issued cautions to English brothers Bobby and Jack Charlton. However, due to Kreitlein not speaking English, the England players learned about the warnings in newspaper accounts and asked for clarification. While driving home one day, the World Cup referee chief, Ken Aston, devised the method of using red and yellow cards to notify players, using traffic lights as his inspiration.

A 4–2 quarterfinal triumph over Peru put Brazil in the semifinals. It also gave Brazil an opportunity to avenge its defeat in the 1950 final against Uruguay. Brazil, needing just a draw against Uruguay to claim the 1950 World Cup on home soil, had lost in a stunning 2–1 game at Maracana.

In 1970, goals by Jairzinho and Rivelino in the final 14 minutes lifted Brazil to a 3–1 win over Uruguay and sent it to the championship match. There, Pelé had the opening goal in a 4–1 victory over Italy. That sealed a sixth win in as many games and a third World Cup title.

Pelé raised the Jules Rimet Trophy for a third time. He had become the first and only player to win three World Cup titles. He had scored 12 goals in four different World Cups and assured his place in soccer history.

Brazil players carry Pelé off the field after the team won the 1970 World Cup in Mexico.

CHAPTER 6

Pelé carries the Jules Rimet Trophy out of Azteca Stadium in Mexico City after Brazil won the 1970 World Cup.

Lured to America

Two months after the 1970 World Cup, Pelé was a father again. His son Edson, or Edinho (little Edson or Edson Jr.) was born on August 27, 1970.

Closing in on his 30th birthday, with no formal education beyond primary school, Pelé began to contemplate his future. With the help of a friend, Julio Mazzei, Pelé studied and passed his secondary education test and entrance exam to get into college for a degree in physical education.

He had spent the past 13 years traveling around the world with both Santos and the Brazilian national team. It was time to slow down and spend more time at home with his wife and two children. Pelé also started to think about retirement, especially from the national team.

Meanwhile in the United States, two Englishmen had arrived with a goal of making soccer there an accepted sport. Clive Toye was the New York Cosmos general manager and Phil Woosnam was the NASL commissioner.

In February 1971, Pelé and Santos were playing an exhibition in Jamaica. Toye, Woosnam, and Kurt Lamm, the general secretary of the USSF, flew to Kingston to meet with Pelé.

"Pelé, I just want you to know that we have a lot of ideas for soccer in the United States," Woosnam told him by a hotel pool, "and you're a part of those ideas."[1] The NASL leaders wanted to suggest to Pelé that he should play for the Cosmos in New York. "Money's no object," Toye told him. "Whatever it takes."[2]

Pelé was only half paying attention and really didn't understand, as Mazzei translated, what New York had to do with him. While already thinking of his future, this was not what he had in mind. He thanked them but said he wasn't interested. He went back to Santos. Toye, Woosnam, and Lamm returned to New York. But Toye had a hunch that the idea intrigued Pelé.

Six months later they met again in Yankee Stadium in New York. The Cosmos were playing the Rochester Lancers in an NASL game and Santos faced Deportivo Cali of Colombia in a doubleheader on August 2. During the day, Toye presented Pelé with a No. 10 Cosmos jersey. In essence he was retiring the number for a player who had never played with the club.

"Big Crocodile"

The game in New York was played less than a month after Pelé had bid farewell to the Brazilian national team in a pair of games. The first was July 11, 1971, against Austria, where he scored his record 77th goal for Brazil in a 1–1 draw. The second game, a week later against Yugoslavia, was a 2–2 draw before 180,000 fans at Maracana with the crowd chanting *"Fica, Fica,"* or "Stay, Stay."

But the travel was wearing on Pelé. Even his attitude toward Santos was deteriorating. His contract

The Cosmos

The original New York Cosmos were the most successful team in the old NASL, winning five championships. The only other team to win more than one title was the Chicago Sting, which won two championships. Turkish immigrant brothers Ahmet and Nesuhi Ertegun and Steve Ross, chairman of Warner Communications, founded the Cosmos in 1971. Ahmet Ertegun had cofounded Atlantic Records, which was absorbed into the Warner Communications conglomerate, the Cosmos corporate owner.

The team hired British immigrant Clive Toye as general manager. Toye chose Brazil's green and yellow for the team's colors with Pelé in mind even though Nesuhi Ertegun wanted to call the team the New York Blues, a nod to his musical tastes. In a "name the team contest," two local school teachers suggested Cosmos, which was short for Cosmopolitans. Toye liked the name. It was similar to one of New York's baseball teams, the Mets, which was short for Metropolitans. Toye's moniker won out.

Pele appears on *The Tonight Show* with Johnny Carson, *right*, in 1973 in New York.

with the team was set to expire at the end of 1972, and he was looking toward the last step in his career. Pelé was still in good form and shape. Santos won the Paulista in 1973 for a tenth time with Pelé, who again was the league's scoring leader.

By 1974, Brazilian officials, including President Emilio Garrastazu, were trying to persuade Pelé to return to the national team for another World Cup. But Pelé was not interested in playing.

Toye also hadn't given up his pursuit of Pelé. In any written correspondence between the Cosmos and Pelé's management officials, such as Mazzei, Pelé was referred to as "Big Crocodile." The code name was used so as to not arouse suspicions.

As the 1974 World Cup approached, Toye discussed signing Pelé with Cosmos owners and Warner Communications executives, brothers Ahmet and Nesuhi Ertegun, and Steve Ross. He told them it would cost $3 million to $4 million for a three-year contract, during which they would have exclusive rights to use Pelé as a marketing icon. They gave their approval. In June, Toye headed to West Germany for the World Cup.

In Frankfurt, Toye met with Pelé and Mazzei. Toye again outlined why Pelé should come to the United States: how he had done everything he could in Brazil but soccer was a novelty in the United States and he could make it explode. But Pelé, although seriously considering retiring from Santos, remained unconvinced. He thanked Toye again, but he was not going to New York.

In August, Toye learned that Pelé was going to fly from Brazil to Canada for a soccer clinic with Pepsi-Cola Co. He arranged to meet with Pelé and Mazzei again

Pelé's Code Name

In the 1970s, cell phones and e-mail did not exist, and secure communications were difficult. To send official letters and correspondence as quickly as possible, devices such as TELEX machines and telecopiers were used. Most offices had one or two machines to send and receive dispatches. But a dispatch could sit in a general distribution box open for anyone to read until given to the person it was intended for. In order to disguise the subject of letters, Julio Mazzei suggested the code name "Big Crocodile" to refer to Pelé. "That sounded as good, and oblique, as any," according to Clive Toye.[3]

at the airport as they waited to change planes in New York. Pelé said no once more. Undaunted, Toye flew to Brazil in September to make his pitch another time, but Pelé still wasn't budging.

Finally, Pelé told Santos he was finished playing. After playing more than 1,200 matches for both Santos and Brazil, he played his last game on October 2 against Ponte Preta. When he left the field, he cried. To him, only weeks shy of his 34th birthday, he was done. He was no longer Pelé; he was Edson.

A Costly Mistake Revisited

His retirement didn't stop the biggest club teams in the world from trying to change his mind. Real Madrid of Spain, Juventus and AC Milan of Italy, and Club America of Mexico, among others, made offers to Pelé. But he was not interested.

However, as 1974 turned into 1975, Pelé found himself in debt again. After the Sanitaria Santista debacle, Pelé rebuilt his finances with the help of his business agent, Marby Ramundini. Pelé set up an office to manage his business interests with advisers and others. They were Mazzei; Pelé's brother Zoca, who had become a lawyer; and an economist named Jose Roberto Ribeiro Xisto.

Xisto had arrived on the scene in 1973 and began cleaning up a financial mess. One problem he couldn't fix, however, was called Fiolax. It was a company that manufactured rubber parts for cars. Pelé owned approximately 6 percent of the company's stock. But he also had signed to back a loan for the company. When the firm couldn't pay, the bank came after Pelé. Besides the loan, Pelé was also responsible for the fines the company owed for violating government regulations. In all, he owed more than a million dollars.

Mazzei, Xisto, Zoca, and Edevar, a former Santos goalkeeper who now was a member of the office staff, approached Pelé about playing for the Cosmos. Mazzei listed 12 reasons for not going to the United States. Among the reasons was that Pelé was likely to face backlash from the Brazilian public who would see him as a traitor. But Mazzei also gave Pelé 18 reasons to go to New York. The biggest reason was the money. It was enough to clear him of debt.

Julio Mazzei

Julio Mazzei and Pelé met in 1965 when Mazzei was hired by Santos FC as its technical instructor. The two became fast friends, and Mazzei became Pelé's most trusted adviser. Known as "The Professor," Mazzei had a degree in physical education from Michigan State University. He had worked for rival club Palmeiras in Sao Paulo before joining Santos. Santos dismissed Mazzei in 1971, adding to Pelé's disillusionment with the team. Pelé, who considered Mazzei a brother and second father, hired him for his office. Mazzei moved to the United States with Pelé and coached the Cosmos in all or part of four seasons, including during the run to the 1982 NASL title.

Considering he could rebuild his financial life again, give his children Kelly and Edinho an educational experience, and be a soccer evangelist in a land virtually untouched by the sport, Pelé became intrigued by the idea of playing in the United States. Now, it was time to call Toye.

His decision was followed by six months of meetings and negotiations in cities around the world in addition to international telephone calls and flights. US Secretary of State Henry Kissinger, who had been born in Germany and was an intense soccer fan, issued a formal invitation to help overcome diplomatic hurdles such as the declaration that made Pelé an unexportable national treasure.

All of it produced a contract with Warner Communications that called for Pelé to play for the Cosmos for three years for $2.8 million. To put it in context, at the time, the highest paid player in Major League Baseball was Hank Aaron. He made $200,000 per season. Pelé's contract also tied him for an additional three years to a Warner subsidiary, Licensing Corporation of America, to use his name for product endorsements.

"It was a very satisfactory contract," Pelé said. "So Rosemeri and I, together with Kelly Cristina and Edinho, came to the United States."[4]

Pelé smiles during an interview in 1975 after signing with the New York Cosmos.

Pelé dribbles the ball during his New York Cosmos debut in a June 15, 1975, exhibition against the Dallas Tornado.

The Cosmos Years

Four days after being introduced as the newest member of the Cosmos at the glitzy press conference in Manhattan, Pelé walked onto the field at Downing Stadium on Randall's Island in the middle of the East River. He was wearing the white No. 10 Cosmos jersey.

It was Sunday, June 15, 1975, and the capacity crowd of 21,278, including actor Robert Redford, strained to see New York's newest celebrity. It was the largest crowd to ever watch a Cosmos home game. Fans could be seen watching the game from the off-ramp of the adjacent Triborough Bridge that towered above the stadium. It was all to watch a hastily arranged exhibition game against the Dallas Tornado. Dallas had arguably the NASL's best-known player, Kyle Rote Jr.

The setting was a stadium built during the Depression in the 1930s that was more than showing its age. The field was a mixture of some grass, a lot of dirt, and rocks. But nothing was going to spoil this debut.

The game was to be televised nationally by the CBS network and to 22 other countries around the world. To make sure it looked good for the TV cameras, some Cosmos staffers had been out early, painting the dirt green.

It had been eight months since Pelé's last game, but considering the quality of most of the players on the Cosmos, he didn't look out of place. However, the game didn't begin the way Pelé had hoped. Dallas took the lead early. By halftime it was 2–0.

Pelé was doing well, and the Cosmos had most of the possession. But Dallas goalkeeper Ken Cooper was having an outstanding game, frustrating New York. Then, 11 minutes into the second half, Pelé played a soft forward ball to Mordechai Shpigler. Shpigler just managed a touch before Cooper could get there. The ball rolled slowly over the goal line for a goal.

Pelé was starting to put on a show. The crowd hit a crescendo every time he touched the ball. Then with 25 minutes left, Pelé leapt above a crowded penalty area and headed in a corner kick for the tying goal. The crowd erupted. Fans ran onto the field and mobbed him.

It was a sign of what was to come. Whenever and wherever Pelé played, the crowds come out in great numbers. Pelé's first official NASL game came three days after the Dallas match. Approximately 22,500 fans showed up at Downing Stadium to watch New York beat the Toronto Metros-Croatia 2–0. Eleven days later, the Cosmos drew a crowd of 35,620 when they played the Diplomats (Dips) in Washington.

The Cosmos had averaged approximately 8,000 fans per game before Pelé showed up in 1975. Afterward, they didn't play before anything smaller than 11,137 until the last four games of the season. Pelé didn't play in those four games as he was hurt with a pulled hamstring.

New York started the season 3–6 without Pelé. The Cosmos then won five of nine. However, they lost two of their last four without Pelé and missed the playoffs.

Like Santos FC, the Cosmos were eager to use the worldwide celebrity of Pelé in off-season foreign tours. They traveled to Europe and the Caribbean after the 1975 NASL season finished.

"Green Fungus"

Most people barely gave the Cosmos or the NASL any attention in the early 1970s. So the team and the league were desperate to show themselves in the best possible light whenever given the chance. For Pelé's debut match on network television, the team had its staff cover the large and numerous dirt areas of the Downing Stadium field with green paint. This led to a rather embarrassing moment for the Cosmos. After the game, Pelé told team president Rafael de la Sierra that he could not play for the team. "All I have is my feet and I have this green fungus growing all over them," Pelé said.[1] De la Sierra had to explain that the "fungus" was actually green paint used to make the field look better.

New Season, More Fame

Pelé's arrival had given soccer enough credibility that other big-name players from Europe also moved to the United States in 1976. Rodney Marsh signed with the Tampa Bay Rowdies. Geoff Hurst joined the Seattle Sounders. Bobby Moore became a member of the San Antonio Thunder. And George Best landed with the Los Angeles Aztecs.

But the biggest name of all was Giorgio Chinaglia. He was the leading scorer on Lazio of the Italian league. Chinaglia joined the Cosmos. Together, he and Pelé formed a potent force. Chinaglia had the second-most goals (19) in the league in 1976. Pelé helped by recording a league-high 18 assists. Pelé also scored 13 goals that year.

By the start of the 1976 season, the team had moved from Downing Stadium back to the much larger Yankee Stadium. The Cosmos averaged 18,571 fans per home game that season. They were a huge draw on the road, too. In Seattle, 58,128 fans came out to see the Cosmos play the Sounders. That was the biggest crowd ever for a soccer game in the United States. The Cosmos beat the Minnesota Kicks 3–1 in Bloomington, Minnesota, before an overflow crowd of 46,164.

In the second half of the season, the Cosmos won six straight. They finished 16–8, second in the Eastern Division behind Tampa Bay. Then New York beat

Pelé celebrates after scoring against the Washington Diplomats during the 1976 NASL playoffs in Yankee Stadium. The Cosmos won the game 2–0.

the Diplomats 2–0 in the first round of the playoffs. However, the Cosmos lost to the Rowdies 3–1 in the second round. Pelé scored in both games.

As the Cosmos' fame grew, so did the tension between Chinaglia and Pelé. Once in the locker room, Chinaglia complained that he wasn't scoring as many goals as he could because he wasn't getting enough passes from Pelé. Pelé responded by saying Chinaglia shot at impossible angles. Regardless, the Cosmos went on another foreign tour, this time to Europe and Japan.

Pelé's Final Year

Many changes came to the Cosmos in 1977, Pelé's final season as a player. For one, the team moved into Giants Stadium. It had been built in the Meadowlands swamps of East Rutherford, New Jersey.

In less than a year, Chinaglia had ingratiated himself with Warner chairman Steve Ross and initiated several personnel moves. Clive Toye resigned. Eddie Firmani, a South African-born Italian, replaced Gordon Bradley as manager. The Cosmos also acquired Germany's most famous player, Franz "Der Kaiser" Beckenbauer. Three years earlier he had led his country to a second World Cup title.

There's No Place Like Home

The New York Cosmos played in three different stadiums before settling at Giants Stadium in 1977 in East Rutherford, New Jersey. They played their first season at old Yankee Stadium in 1971, moved to Hofstra (University) Stadium in 1972, then Downing Stadium in 1974, before going back to Yankee Stadium in 1976.

Downing Stadium opened in 1936 and was a dilapidated wreck by the time the Cosmos arrived. The paint was peeling, and the concrete was crumbling. On the telecast of Pelé's first game, CBS sportscaster Jack Whitaker called it, "A sandlot . . . in a city of glass and steel."[2] The stadium sat on Randall's Island in the middle of New York City's East River. It was named after John J. Downing, a director in New York's Department of Parks and Recreation.

Of all the places the Cosmos played, only Hofstra Stadium was still standing in 2013. Downing Stadium was demolished in 2002. Giants Stadium and Yankee Stadium were razed in 2010.

Beckenbauer arrived nine games into the season. After an initial loss, the Cosmos went on a five-game winning streak. Meanwhile, the Cosmos became even more popular. Home or away, they drew crowds of 45,000 at Tampa, 62,319 at home against the Rowdies, and 57,000 at home against Los Angeles. Rock stars such as Mick Jagger of the Rolling Stones visited the locker room. So did actors and actresses, such as Robert Redford and Barbra Streisand, and superstars from other sports such as heavyweight boxing champion Muhammad Ali.

Studio 54

Called the most famous nightclub in the world during its heyday from 1977 to 1980, Studio 54 was a discotheque that was notorious for its clientele of celebrities and drugs. It was located on West 54th Street in Manhattan. The club gained fame quickly for its multimedia visual effects. Its popularity declined after the original owners sold the club, although it still operated as a nightclub into the 1990s. The building has since been converted into a theater.

The Cosmos were bona fide celebrities, with tables reserved for them at New York's famous Studio 54 nightclub. Pelé and Chinaglia were the lead attractions.

Soccer had exploded into popularity so much that ABC sportscaster Howard Cosell predicted that it would surpass professional football and baseball.

But Pelé still needed a championship to cement his legacy, and his teammates seemed determined to win one for him. Carlos Alberto, Pelé's teammate from Brazil's 1970 World Cup team, was added to the squad with four games remaining. That proved to be the final element for a championship run. The Cosmos lost only one of their remaining regular-season games. Then they won six straight playoff games, including an 8–3 rout over the Fort Lauderdale Strikers at Giants Stadium in front of a record crowd of 77,691.

The Soccer Bowl championship game was almost a formality. The Cosmos beat the Seattle Sounders 2–1 in Portland, Oregon. Pelé again was lifted onto the shoulders of his teammates and carried off the field. It would not be the last time, though.

He and the Cosmos made another foreign tour, this one to Latin America, Japan, and China. Then he played a final farewell game on October 1, 1977, at Giants Stadium. A worldwide audience watched on television.

Pelé played the first half for the Cosmos, scoring a goal. Then he played the second half for Santos in a 2–1 New York victory. Pelé had finished his career with a record 1,281 goals.

"I . . . felt that I had played my part in what I had set out to do," Pelé said about retiring just three weeks before his thirty-seventh birthday. "Football had really caught on in the US."[3]

It would not last, however. The NASL would die out by 1985. Yet Pelé and the league still left a legacy for soccer's future in the United States.

Pelé controls the ball while playing in his farewell match with the
New York Cosmos on October 1, 1977, at Giants Stadium.

CHAPTER 8

Pelé instructs young soccer players during a clinic at New York's Madison Square Garden in 1978.

Life after Soccer

Pelé hadn't even retired when the post-career accolades began to roll in. Four days before his farewell game at Giants Stadium, the United Nations (UN) declared him "A Citizen of the World." In short order, he was also named Goodwill Ambassador for UNICEF, the UN's children's charity.

FIFA selected him to join its Fair Play Committee, which encourages attractive play and good sportsmanship. It was not a huge surprise since Pelé had campaigned for fellow Brazilian Joao Havelange when he ran for and won the presidency of FIFA in 1974.

After his initial contract expired, Pelé signed a 10-year extension with Warner Communications for it to continue representing his commercial rights. But the 1978 World Cup offered him his first opportunity at a soccer career beyond being a player. He traveled to Argentina to be a television commentator, but the job came at a high cost.

His third child, Jennifer, was born while he was away at the tournament. That was a final straw that angered his wife Rosemeri irreparably. Pelé said his time away, as much as eight months every year over the nearly two previous decades, was too much. Rosemeri wanted a divorce. That was not the first painful moment in their marriage.

Pelé had fathered two daughters with other women. The first was born in 1964, two years before he was married but after he had started dating Rosemeri. The other was born in 1968, a year after Rosemeri gave birth to Kelly Cristina.

Rosemeri and Pelé separated a week after Jennifer's birth. Their divorce became final later that year. Rosemeri returned home to Brazil after Pelé's playing career ended. He remained in New York and continued to enjoy his time in the spotlight.

The popularity that soccer enjoyed after Pelé arrived in the United States created a new opportunity for him: the movies. He had been in four films before, twice playing himself, but in 1981 he was given a chance to appear in a major Hollywood production. Thanks to his connections with Warner Communications, Pelé was asked to be one of the headline attractions in *Victory*, or *Escape to Victory* as it was known in other parts of the world.

Pelé poses with Argentina star Diego Maradona, *left*, and France star Michel Platini, *right*, at a 1988 celebration match for Platini.

The movie starred Sylvester Stallone and Michael Caine. It told the story of a bunch of Allied prisoners of war who took on the German national team during World War II in an exhibition match in Paris.

Pelé played a corporal from Trinidad & Tobago who scores the equalizing goal from a signature bicycle

Two Daughters

Pelé initially learned of his first out-of-wedlock child, Sandra Regina Machado, in 1967. Her mother was Anisia Machado, the maid who cleaned Pelé's house when he played with Santos FC. Anisia brought Sandra to Pelé's house, but he denied he was her father. Wide attention to her claim didn't come until 1993 when a DNA test proved he was her father. Sandra sued and won the right to use his last name and later wrote a book titled *The Daughter the King Didn't Want*. Sandra died of cancer in 2006 at 42. Pelé also fathered another girl from an affair with a reporter, Lenita Kurtz. Flavia Christina Kurtz, however, did not sue and remains on good terms with her father.

kick. Numerous soccer stars of the day were in the film. Among those stars were Bobby Moore of England, Osvaldo Ardiles of Argentina, and Paul Van Himst of Belgium. One of Pelé's teammates from his Cosmos years, captain Werner Roth, played the star of the German team.

More Notoriety

Pelé might have been less visible in a business suit than a soccer uniform, but he was still a celebrity. He dated models and beauty queens, including teenager Maria da Graca Meneghel, or Xuxa. She later posed for *Playboy* magazine before taking over as the host of a children's show in Brazil.

Pelé eventually married again in April 1994. His new wife was psychologist and gospel music singer Assiria Seixas Lemos. Two and a half years later, she gave birth to twins, Joshua and Celeste. But that marriage also ended in divorce in 2008.

Other personal tragedies hounded Pelé and his family. His son Edinho had become a goalkeeper and played with four different Brazilian teams, including Santos. However, beginning in 1992 he got into various legal troubles. Edinho was involved in an illegal street race in which a motorcyclist was struck and killed. He later was arrested twice on drug-trafficking charges and went to a rehabilitation clinic for marijuana addiction.

There was also more turmoil in Pelé's business life. In 1990, he created Pelé Sports & Marketing (PS&M). The company would not only manage his personal image and endorsement contracts but also invest in television and marketing events. He put the company in the hands of Celso Grellet, an experienced professional in Brazilian sports marketing, and Helio Viana, whom Pelé had met while Viana was working for the mayor of Rio de Janeiro.

Within years, the company became embroiled in scandal when it attempted to purchase the television rights for the 1994 Brazilian national league championship. Pelé did not attend the meeting

Pelé's Other Son

Pelé's son Edinho received considerable attention for his arrests and drug addiction rather than his soccer career. But Pelé's younger son, Joshua Nascimento, from his second wife Assiria Lemos, also has taken to the game. He played two years for the Florida Rush youth club in Ocoee, an organization designated by the USSF as one of its Developmental Academy teams. Joshua joined his father's old club and made his debut on the Santos U-17 team in early 2013.

but was told by his associates that CBF officials had demanded a $1 million bribe. Pelé was outraged and publicly accused the CBF of corruption in a 1993 *Playboy* interview.

The accusation created a firestorm, starting a personal war of words between Pelé and CBF President Ricardo Teixeira. Because of the controversy, FIFA did not officially invite Pelé to the 1994 World Cup in the United States. Havelange, the head of FIFA at the time, was Teixeira's father-in-law. Pelé felt especially hurt by the snub since he had done so much to bring the World Cup to the United States.

Pelé later learned that the bribe demands were not true, and he apologized. But it wasn't until 2001 when he and Brazilian soccer officials called a truce.

PS&M and the Pelé Law

Perhaps the biggest mess came in 1995. PS&M obtained a $700,000 loan to stage a charity game between European and South American all-stars. But the game was canceled and the bank loan wasn't repaid. Pelé had the company audited and said he suspected Viana of stealing as much as $10 million. Viana was later accused by a Brazilian parliamentary investigation of five crimes related to the scandal. But the damage to Pelé's reputation was enormous.

Although badly damaged, Pelé's name wasn't completely destroyed. He closed PS&M. After twice rebuffing offers to go into politics, Pelé accepted an appointment as minister of sport in the Brazilian government from President Fernando Henrique Cardoso in 1995.

Having played the game for a living, Pelé despised the idea of a player being bound to a club for life. He proposed bringing the concept of free agency to Brazilian athletes. The Pelé Law passed in 1998. Among other things, the law allowed players to leave a club after their contracts had expired without owing compensation to the team.

Free Agency

Until the late 1900s, professional athletes throughout the world were considered the property of a team when they signed a contract. Those contracts gave the club exclusive rights to a player even after the contract had expired under what was referred to in American sports as the "reserve clause." The clause gave teams the sole right to terminate the contract. That changed in the United States in 1975 when baseball players Andy Messersmith and Dave McNally challenged the system and won. After their contracts expired, they were called "free agents," able to sign with whatever club they chose. European athletes had their moment in 1995 when Belgian player Jean-Marc Bosman similarly sued in the European Court of Justice against his team, RFC Liege, the Belgian Football Association, and the Union of European Football Associations (UEFA). Some form of free agency is standard in most professional sports leagues today.

Other provisions of the law forced sports teams, many of which were run as amateur social clubs, to operate as regular businesses. That included having to pay taxes and observe standard accounting practices. The Pelé Law also broke the monopoly the CBF had on organizing and running leagues and tournaments. This allows clubs to make agreements among themselves.

It was a bitter struggle to pass the proposals. The teams vigorously opposed the new rules. They invested a lot of money into developing players and argued they could lose them for nothing. The teams also fought the idea of being treated as a regular business.

The CBF, too, opposed the measures, which came during the same time Pelé and Teixeira were feuding. Pelé resigned as minister of sport after the law was passed. The Brazilian government in 2001 weakened many of the disputed provisions. But free agency remained, and Pelé had another victory.

Despite the Pelé Law, his post-playing days left a legacy as a negligent businessman. Legal fees to clean up investment disasters required him to continue his promotional work by lending his name to companies.

"The whole PS&M fiasco cost me a packet and still takes up time and money because of my legal action against Hélio Viana," Pelé wrote in a 2006 autobiography. "One of the reasons why I still have to work so hard is that I have so many lawyers to pay."[1]

Pelé, then Brazil's sports minister, celebrates in front of the cathedral in Brasilia, Brazil, after the Pelé Law passed the Brazilian senate in 1998.

CHAPTER 9

Pelé, *center*, and former Santos FC teammates hold up the Libertadores championship trophy in 2012 during the club's centennial celebration.

International Acclaim and Legacy

P elé played professional soccer for two decades, but his dominance of the game during that span left an impact that lasts to this day. The honors and awards given to him read like a laundry list: The international news service Reuters and the International Olympic Committee chose him as the greatest Athlete of the Century in 1999; French magazine *L'Equipe* did the same in 1981; UNICEF and *France Football* magazine dubbed him Football Player of the Century in 1999; FIFA elected him Player of the Century in 2000.

The fame he had earned as a player opened doors to movie and television roles, government jobs, and countless product endorsements. Pepsi, MasterCard, and Viagra were some of his most famous associations. He still works as a television commentator for soccer events. In 2012, he hired the New York firm Legends 10 to manage his endorsements.

Pelé and Maradona

As someone who is always included in the discussion of the greatest player of all time, Pelé has most often been compared to Argentina's Diego Maradona. The comparisons have only led to a bitter exchange of insults between the two. Pelé has referred to Maradona as a negative example because of his many well-publicized bouts with drug abuse. Maradona countered on more than one occasion by accusing Pelé of engaging in homosexual acts.

He is the benchmark by which all other players are judged. When new players appear on the soccer scene, the comparisons to Pelé are inevitable. Ronaldo, Robinho, David Beckham, Wayne Rooney, Lionel Messi, and Neymar all have been analyzed and contrasted with the player who was called "The King" and "The Black Pearl." He was and is known around the world. Rohit Brijnath wrote in Singapore's *The Straits Times* in 2011:

Nothing of Pelé was forgotten because so little of Pelé was known growing up in Asia. . . . When I called my father to tell him Pelé was arriving here, he, 75, said without hesitation: 'Ah, Edson Arantes Do Nascimento.' [sic]

In a way, Pelé—along with his contemporary Muhammad Ali—is among the last of sports' truly mythical figures. The Brazilian was larger than life, he seemed to waltz out of a boy's comic book and arrived from a non-invasive time when we believed our heroes could actually hurdle tall buildings.[1]

Pele's legacy as an ambassador for Brazil continued into the 2010s. He helped his country win the rights to host the 2014 World Cup. He was also on the team that successfully bid to host the 2016 Olympic Games in Rio de Janeiro. South America had never hosted an Olympic Games.

NASL Legacy

Pelé never went into coaching after retiring. Instead, his playing career made an impact beyond the game.

Seven years after he walked off the field at Giants Stadium, the NASL played its last game in 1984. The league had started conducting camps and clinics for kids in the early 1970s before Pelé's debut. But his arrival in the United States with the Cosmos sparked a surge of interest.

Players such as Franz Beckenbauer, Johan Neeskens, Carlos Alberto, George Best, and countless

Demise of the NASL

Pelé retired from the Cosmos and the NASL in 1977. Within seven years, both were extinct. Analysts have debated the cause for decades. But some of the reasons were tied to Pelé. The influx of soccer stars like Pelé and Franz Beckenbauer raised the league's profile quickly. Warner Communications, owner of the Cosmos, could absorb million-dollar losses because it used the team to promote its other businesses, such as its music and film divisions. Without such corporate backing, other teams could not afford the losses. Television and sponsorship revenue couldn't cover the costs to run the teams. When Warner's Atari game sales plummeted in the early 1980s, it no longer could afford the team and disbanded it in 1984.

others followed and heightened the popularity of soccer even further, particularly among children.

Soccer Grows in the United States

Mike Windischmann was a ball boy for the Cosmos, and his youth team was at the airport to greet Beckenbauer when he arrived in the United States. Thirteen years later, in 1990, Windischmann captained the United States to its first World Cup in 40 years.

Major League Soccer

MLS was specifically designed to avoid the problems that afflicted the NASL. It started in 1996 under a financial organization it calls "single entity." Major League Baseball, the National Football League, the National Basketball Association, and the National Hockey League all began when teams got together in a relatively loose affiliation to play games. In MLS, individuals or groups invest in the league and are given rights to operate a team in a specific city. MLS, not the teams, pay the players' salaries and each team must adhere to a salary budget. This prohibits one team, like the Cosmos, from outspending the others.

The players challenged single entity. They sued the league claiming it created an illegal monopoly. The players lost the case in 2000 and single entity remains.

The conservative business model helped MLS survive difficult times in its early years. However, the league saw great growth after allowing teams to spend more money on designated players in 2007. When English star David Beckham signed with the Los Angeles Galaxy that year, many compared it to Pelé's arrival with the Cosmos years earlier. As of 2013, MLS had 19 teams.

England's David Beckham, one of the most famous soccer players in the world, followed Pelé in 2007 by coming to the United States to play in MLS.

The seed sown by Pelé had started to bear fruit. Four years later, in 1994, three players who grew up watching Pelé and the Cosmos—John Harkes, Tab Ramos, and Tony Meola—led the American team into the second round of the World Cup.

The United States was awarded the 1994 World Cup with the provision that the country restart a first-division professional league. By 1996, MLS had started with 10 teams and a generation of players who

The Cosmos Today

Although the team last played in the NASL in 1984, a New York Cosmos team was reborn in 2010. After the Cosmos ceased to play as a team, the club's last general manager, Pepe Pinton, kept the name alive. He used it to operate clinics and soccer camps. In 2010, Pinton sold the rights to a group headed by Paul Kemsley, who announced plans to return the Cosmos to competitive play. The team named Pelé as its honorary president. The club first fielded a U-23 team in the Premier Development League, a semi-pro/ amateur division, in 2011. The club began play in 2013 in a similarly reborn North American Soccer League, which is now the second tier of American soccer under MLS.

had watched and been inspired by Pelé, the Cosmos, and the NASL. In 2002, the United States reached the quarterfinals of the World Cup.

Similarly, a generation of women players such as Mia Hamm grew up watching the NASL and Pelé. The United States won the inaugural Women's World Cup in 1991 and went on to win it again in 1999. That is in addition to four of five Olympic gold medals since women's soccer was introduced into the Games in 1996.

"In effect, Pelé overnight turned this fringe activity we called soccer into something central in American life," Clive Toye said. "Until it grew and grew into what it is today."[2]

Pelé scored 1,281 goals in his career and is the only player to win three World Cups.

TIMELINE

1940

Edson Arantes do Nascimento is born in Três Corações, Brazil. The government recognizes his birthday as October 21.

1956

Pelé joins Santos FC. He plays his first game and scores his first goal for Santos on September 7.

1957

Pelé signs his first official contract with Santos on April 8.

1958

Pelé wins the first of 10 Paulista titles with Santos.

1960

Pelé wins his first of six Brazilian national league championships with Santos.

1962

Pelé plays in the first two games of the World Cup, but injury keeps him out after that as Brazil wins its second consecutive title.

1957

Pelé scores 17 goals in the Sao Paulo state championship, which is also known as the Paulista.

1957

Pelé makes his Brazilian national team debut and scores a goal on July 7.

1958

Pelé scores six goals, including two in the final against host Sweden, to lead Brazil to its first World Cup title.

1964

Pelé fathers a daughter, Sandra Machado, out of wedlock. Later he denies parentage until a test in 1993 proves it.

1965

Pelé's investment, building materials company Sanitiria Santista, goes bankrupt, forcing Pelé to seek help from Santos to pay off debt.

1966

Pelé marries Rosemeri dos Reis Cholbi.

TIMELINE

1969

Pelé scores his 1,000th goal in a 2–1 Santos victory over Vasco da Gama on November 19.

1970

Pelé scores four goals to lead Brazil to an unprecedented third World Cup title in Mexico.

1971

In February, Clive Toye, Phil Woosnam, and Kurt Lamm meet with Pelé in Kingston, Jamaica.

1977

The Cosmos win the NASL championship 2–1 over the Seattle Sounders on August 28 in Pelé's final competitive game.

1977

On October 1, Pelé plays a farewell match at Giants Stadium before a capacity crowd and international television audience.

1994

Pelé marries for a second time, to Assiria Seixas Lemos, but they get divorced in 2008.

1974

Pelé plays his last
game for Santos on
October 2.

1975

Another company
Pelé has invested
in, Fiolax, goes
bankrupt.

1975

Pelé signs with the
New York Cosmos.
He is introduced to
the New York press
corps on June 10.

1995

PS&M becomes
embroiled in
scandal involving
a charity game.
An audit reveals
mismanagement
and the company is
dissolved.

1995

Pelé becomes the
Brazilian minister of
sport.

1998

The Pelé Law is
enacted in Brazil,
essentially creating
free agency for
athletes in the
country.

DATE OF BIRTH
October 23, 1940 (officially: October 21, 1940)

PLACE OF BIRTH
Três Corações, Brazil

PARENTS
Dona Celeste Arantes, Joao Ramos do Nascimento (Dondinho)

EDUCATION
Fourth grade; secondary diploma (GED equivalent); degree, Faculdade de Educacao Fisica (Faculty of Physical Education), Santos University

MARRIAGES
Rosemeri dos Reis Cholbi,1966 (divorced, 1978)
Assiria Seixas Lemos,1994 (divorced, 2008)

CHILDREN
With Anisia Machado:
Sandra Regina Machado, 1964

With Rosemeri dos Reis Cholbi:
Kelly Cristina, 1967; Edson (Edinho), 1970; Jennifer, 1978

With Lenita Kurtz:
Flavia Christina Kurtz, 1968

With Assiria Lemos Seixas:
Joshua and Celeste (twins), 1996

CAREER HIGHLIGHTS

Pelé is the only man to win the World Cup three times, having done so with Brazil in 1958, 1962, and 1970. By unofficial accounts, he has scored either 1,281 (FIFA) or 1,283 goals (his own count). FIFA does not consider its count to be a record, but nobody has claimed to be close. Pelé led both Brazil and Santos FC to unprecedented heights. His move to the United States met with similar success as he led the New York Cosmos to the 1977 NASL title.

SOCIAL CONTRIBUTIONS

Pelé is largely credited with sparking the surge in popularity and success of soccer in the United States. His move to play with the New York Cosmos in 1975 generated unprecedented publicity that led to waves of youth participation. In his post-playing days, Pelé became minister of sport in the Brazilian government, responsible for creating the Pelé Law, which gave players some measure of what Americans refer to as free agency.

CONFLICTS

Pelé initially denied fathering a daughter, Sandra Machado, with a maid in 1964. Machado sued Pelé to prove she was his daughter. Professionally, when Pelé formed his business PS&M he initially made claims that the CBF was corrupt, saying it had demanded bribes from him for a television contract. He eventually recanted the accusation. PS&M later was embroiled in a scandal of its own, defaulting on payments and accused of stealing money intended to stage a charity game.

QUOTE

"And I could help the game of football there; Toye had said so and he meant it, and I agreed."—*Pelé*

GLOSSARY

club

A soccer team made up of players regardless of nationality, such as Santos FC.

commissioner

The chief executive of a sports league.

contract

A binding agreement between a player and a company or team that determines things such as salary and length of commitment between the two parties.

cup

Often used to refer to a tournament, such as the World Cup, or English FA Cup. The term derives from the trophies that are given to the winner, often a cup-like statuette.

endorsements

Agreements between a company and a famous person for that person to use and promote the company's products in exchange for payment.

equalize

To tie a game with a goal. An equalizer is the goal that ties a game.

friendly

An exhibition soccer match.

header

To pass or shoot the ball using the head.

manager

The head coach of a soccer team.

marking

To defend against another player individually.

national team
    A team made up of players solely from one country that
    represents the country in a tournament, competition,
    or game.

selectors
    Individuals, usually coaches or scouts, who help a head coach
    or manager choose—or select—players for a roster.

semiprofessional
    A person who receives some money for playing but not
    enough to earn a living.

side
    A club or team.

Soccer Bowl
    The name given to the championship game of the NASL from
    1975 to 1984, after which the league folded. The term was
    derived from American football's Super Bowl.

tour
    A series of exhibition games played away from home either
    to prepare a team for a tournament or season or to make
    extra money.

transfer
    The primary way in which soccer players move from one club
    team to another, most often by having their contract sold.

trap
    A method in which a soccer player controls a ball passed to
    him or her.

RESOURCES

SELECTED BIBLIOGRAPHY

Once in a Lifetime: The Extraordinary Story of the New York Cosmos. Dirs.: Paul Crowder, John Dower. Miramax Films, GreeneStreet Films, 2006. Film.

Pelé, with Orlando Duarte and Alex Bellos. Translated from Portuguese by Daniel Hahn. *Pelé: The Autobiography.* London: Simon & Schuster UK, 2006. Print.

Toye, Clive. *A Kick in the Grass.* Haworth, NJ: St. Johann Press, 2006. Print.

FURTHER READINGS

Kuper, Simon. *Soccer Men: Profiles of the Rogues, Geniuses and Neurotics Who Dominate the World's Most Popular Sport.* New York: Nation Books, 2011. Print.

McDougall, Chrös. *Soccer.* Minneapolis, MN: ABDO Publishing Co., 2012. Print.

Monnig, Alex. *The World Cup.* Minneapolis, MN: ABDO Publishing Co., 2013. Print.

Wahl, Grant. *The Beckham Experiment: How the World's Most Famous Athlete Tried to Conquer America.* New York: Crown Publishing Group, 2009. Print.

WEB LINKS

To learn more about Pelé, visit ABDO Publishing Company online at **www.abdopublishing.com**. Web sites about Pelé are featured on our Book Links page. These links are routinely monitored and updated to provide the most current information available.

PLACES TO VISIT

Brazilian Soccer Museum
(Museo do Futebol)
Praça Charles Miller
S/N - Estádio do Pacaembu, Sao Paulo, 01234-010 Brasil
(55) 11 3664-3848
www.museudofutebol.org.br/?lang=en
Located underneath the grandstands of Paulo Machado de Carvalho Municipal Stadium—otherwise known as the Pacaembu Stadium—the museum traces the sport of soccer in Brazil. Instead of artifacts, the museum is more representations of players, clubs and associations, and supporters. It presents facts about Brazilian culture and society in the 1900s.

Lockhart Stadium
1350 NW 55th Street, Fort Lauderdale, FL 33309
754-321-1200
www.strikers.com
Built in 1959, Lockhart Stadium has been the home to four professional or semiprofessional soccer teams, three of them called the Fort Lauderdale Strikers. The first Strikers team, from 1977 to 1983, lost a 3–0 game in Lockhart in 1977 in which Pelé, Giorgio Chinaglia, and Franz Beckenbauer all scored.

CHAPTER 1. The Day US Soccer Changed

1. David Hirshey. "When Soccer Ruled the USA." *E-Ticket.* ESPN Internet Ventures, 5 July 2006. Web. 7 Sept. 2013.

2. Pelé, with Robert Fish. *Pelé: My Life and the Beautiful Game.* New York: Doubleday, 1977. Print. 292.

3. Brian Trusdell. "Those Who Remember Say Beckham's Arrival Can't Compare to Pelé's." *U-T San Diego.* San Diego Union-Tribune, 18 Jan. 2007. Web. 7 Sept. 2013.

4. Pelé, with Robert Fish. *Pelé: My Life and the Beautiful Game.* New York: Doubleday, 1977. Print. 287.

CHAPTER 2. What's in a Name?

1. Pelé, with Orlando Duarte and Alex Bellos. Translated from Portuguese by Daniel Hahn. *Pelé: The Autobiography.* London: Simon & Schuster UK, 2006. Print. 14.

2. Pelé, with Robert Fish. *Pelé: My Life and the Beautiful Game.* New York: Doubleday, 1977. Print. 25.

3. Ibid. 26.

CHAPTER 3. To Sao Paulo, Santos, and Sweden

1. Pelé, with Orlando Duarte and Alex Bellos. Translated from Portuguese by Daniel Hahn. *Pelé: The Autobiography.* London: Simon & Schuster UK, 2006. Print. 72.

2. Ibid. 93.

CHAPTER 4. Making Santos into a Power

1. Pelé, with Orlando Duarte and Alex Bellos. Translated from Portuguese by Daniel Hahn. *Pelé: The Autobiography.* London: Simon & Schuster UK, 2006. Print. 111.

CHAPTER 5. Cementing a Legacy

1. Pelé, with Robert Fish. *Pelé: My Life and the Beautiful Game.* New York: Doubleday, 1977. Print. 169.

2. Pelé, with Orlando Duarte and Alex Bellos. Translated from Portuguese by Daniel Hahn. *Pelé: The Autobiography.* London: Simon & Schuster UK, 2006. Print. 178.

3. Ibid. 131.

4. Ibid. 150.

5. Ian Morrison. *The World Cup: A Complete Record 1930–1990.* Derby, UK: Breedon Books Sport, 1990. Print. 200.

CHAPTER 6. Lured to America

1. Peter Bodo and David Hirshey, with Pelé. *Pelé's New World*. New York: W.W. Norton & Company, 1977. Print. 55.

2. Pelé, with Orlando Duarte and Alex Bellos. Translated from Portuguese by Daniel Hahn. *Pelé: The Autobiography*. London: Simon & Schuster UK, 2006. Print. 205.

3. Clive Toye. Personal interview. 2 May 2013.

4. Pelé, with Robert Fish. *Pelé: My Life and the Beautiful Game*. New York: Doubleday, 1977. Print. 289.

CHAPTER 7. The Cosmos Years

1. Adam Shergold. "Twice in a Lifetime." *Mail Online*. Associated Newspapers, 29 July 2013. Web. 7 Sept. 2013.

2. "Dallas Tornado vs. New York Cosmos." *CBS Sports Spectacular*. CBS Sports, 15 June 1975. DVD.

3. Pelé, with Orlando Duarte and Alex Bellos. Translated from Portuguese by Daniel Hahn. *Pelé: The Autobiography*. London: Simon & Schuster UK, 2006. Print. 233.

CHAPTER 8. Life after Soccer

1. Pelé, with Orlando Duarte and Alex Bellos. Translated from Portuguese by Daniel Hahn. *Pelé: The Autobiography.* London: Simon & Schuster UK, 2006. Print. 292.

CHAPTER 9. International Acclaim and Legacy

1. Rohit Brijnath. "Pelé, Myth and Magic from an Era Gone By." *The Straights Times* (Singapore), 2 March 2011. *LexisNexis.* Web. 7 Sept. 2013.

2. Clive Toye. Personal interview. 2 May 2013.

INDEX

ABOUT THE AUTHOR

Brian Trusdell has covered soccer for more than three decades, beginning with the Pittsburgh Spirit in the old Major Indoor Soccer League. He has worked for the Associated Press and Bloomberg, reporting and editing from four World Cups and six Olympic Games. He has covered both the US men's and women's national teams since 1985 and has reported on MLS from the moment it was officially announced. He also was the executive editor at CONCACAF, the regional governing body for soccer in North America, Central America, and the Caribbean.

PHOTO CREDITS